Dikter Svenska Arabiska Engelska

Dikter.

Svenska Arabiska Engelska

Anna Enbom

© 2023 Anna Enbom
Förlag: BoD – Books on Demand, Stockholm, Sverige
Tryck: BoD – Books on Demand, Norderstedt, Tyskland
ISBN: 978-91-8027-028-1

Tack vare arabiskan upptäckte jag poesi.

Jag framför mina dikter på scener runtom i Sverige på såväl svenska som arabiska. Jag översätter vänners och döda poeters verk från arabiska till svenska. Med hjälp av vänner översätter jag från svenska till arabiska.

På sidorna 7–47 kan du läsa några av mina dikter på både svenska och arabiska.

*

För att hålla igång skrivandet deltar jag i National Poetry Writing Month (NaPoWriMo). Under april månad skriver jag en dikt om dagen på engelska. En del av dem kan du läsa på sidorna 49–83.

*

Förutom dikter skriver jag noveller och romaner.
Två av mina noveller har har vunnit priser.
Du hittar flera av mina texter på annaenbom.se

Dikter på svenska och arabiska

Svenska är mitt modersmål men det är arabiska jag älskar.

Här följer ett urval av mina dikter.
Varje dikt finns på svenska och arabiska.
Stort tack till min vän Maan Haidar som har hjälpt till med
översättningen.

Jag har byggt webbplatsen arabic.fi
Där lär jag ut arabiska till över 30 000 användare i månaden.
Bland annat kan besökarna studera arabiska via dikter.

Fler av mina tvåspråkiga dikter finns på annaenbom.se/poem

Jag gräver
med bara fötter
och jordiga knän.

Jag skyfflar
med händerna.
Jag skopar
med tänderna.

Jag kan inte flyga
så jag gräver
efter mask.

Det är det enda
jag kan göra för
att på något vis
känna mig fri
som en fågel.

أحفِرُ
حافية القدمينِ
موحلة الرّكبتينِ

أغرِف بِيديَّ
أجرِّف بِأسناني

لا أستطيع أن أطير
فأُنَقِّبُ الأرض
عن الدودِ

أحسُدُ الطيور
التي تُحَلِّقُ حرّةً
في السماء

لا أستطيع أن أطير
فأحفِرُ بالأرضِ
هذا كلّ ما يُمكِنُني فِعلَه
كي أشعر
نوعا ما
أنّني حرّ كالطيرِ

Du ser på naturen
på samma sätt som
du ser på mig
Du vill gräva upp blommorna
och ordna dem i räta rader
Du vill slipa trädstammarna raka
kapa kronorna så att varje björk
uppvisar samma höjd

أنت تنظر إلى الطبيعة
كما تنظر إليّ
تريد أن تقلع الأزهار
لكي تزرعها مرتّبةً في خطوط مستقيمة
تريد أن تقشّر جذوع الأشجار
لكي تصبح مستويةً
وتقطع قممها
لكي تكون كلها
بطول واحد

Resväskan stod mitt i vardagsrummet.
Hjulen var svarta och glänsande, utan rispor från asfalt.
Jag packade en baddräkt. Vi gjorde planer.
Snart. Till hösten. När projektet är klart.

Jag packade flipflops.
Föräldrar behövde hjälp, vänner krävde hjälp.
Efter vintern. Till påsk.

Jag bredde ut en handduk på golvet, den blommiga.
Satte på mig en solhatt.
Jag sa: "Vi behöver ingen strand, bara vi är tillsammans."
Jag höll din handled, greppade den som en handklov
för att den inte skulle försvinna.
Memorerade med fingrarna: värmen, de sträva hårstråna.
Du sa: "Nu måste jag till kontoret."
Resväskan ställdes i hörnet.
Snart, till hösten, nästa år.

Jag sa. "Det gör inget, bara vi är tillsammans."
Resan blev aldrig av. Väskan stod kvar.
Jag klarade inte att packa upp den.
Jag försökte minnas värmen från din handled.

كانت الحقيبة في وسط غرفة الجلوس
كانت عجلاتها سوداء ولامعة وبدون أخداش من الطريق
حزمتُ مايّوهي
خطّطنا الرِحلة
عمّا قريب
في فصلِ الخريف
عندما نكمل المشروع

حزمتُ صندلي
كان الوالدون يحتاجون إلى مساعدتنا
كان الأصدقاء يطلبون مساعدتنا
بعد الشّتاء
في فصلِ الربيعِ

وضعتُ منشفة مزهرة على أرض غرفة الجلوس
ارتديتُ قبّعة القشّ
"قلتُ: "لا نحتاج إلى شاطئ. أهمّ شيء هو أنّنا سويّا
لمستُ معصمكَ شديدا كأنّ يدي صفد لأنّني خفتُ أنّك ستختفي
حافظت أصابعي جلدكَ. حافظت حرارتكَ وشعركَ الخشن
"قلتَ: "لازم أن أذهب إلى مكتبي
وضعنا الحقيبة في ركنِ غرفة الجلوسِ
عمّا قريب
في الفصلِ الخريف
في السنة القادمة

"قلتُ: "لا توجد مشكلة, أهمّ شيءٍ هو أنّنا سويّا
لم نسافر
بقيت الحقيبة في الغرفة. لم أقدر أن أفرغها
حاولتُ أن أتذكّر حرارة معصمكَ

Där går hon
i brokiga kläder
tre storlekar för stora
från tre olika dödsbon
köpta på loppis för tre tior
kring henne skramlar
kassar med pantburkar
skorna läcker in
hon snubblar nästan
på byxtyget som böljar
likt svepkläderna på
en grekisk gud

تمشي هناك

ملابسها ملونة متنافرة

ثلاثة مقاسات أكبر من قياسها

اشتريتها بثلاثين كرونة

في ثلاثة أسواق البالة

تقرقع حولها علبات فارغة

التي جمعتها لتعيدها إلى الدكان

لكي تَكسِبَ بعضَ الكرونات

حذاؤها مهتريء

تتعثَّر بقماش سروالها

الذي يرفرف

مثل أزياء إله يوناني

Högarna med grånat
gräsklipp liknade
vid första anblicken
flockar av fåglar
Sen flög fåglarna
och gräshögarna
låg orörliga kvar
När fåglarna flugit
syntes inget liv
och jag anade att
jag var dödare
än gräshögarna
De skingras snart
lämnar småstadens
kommunala gräsplan
medan jag blir kvar

الأكوام بالعشب المقطوع

شبهت لأول وهلة

أسرابا من الطيور

ثم طارت الطيور

وبقيت أكوام الأعشب

جامدة

ولم تُوجد في المكان

أي أثار من الحياة

ففهمتُ أنّني ميتة

أكثر من أكوام الأعشب

ألأكوام تتنشّر عمّا قريب

وتترك المساحة العشبية قاحلةً

بينما سأبقى هنا إلى الأبد

Jag minns rutan snarare än utsikten.
Den var fläckig.
Jag minns att jag tittade på husen på andra sidan vägen.
Jag tyckte synd om de som bodde där, så nära.
Jag minns en fotbollsplan.
Jag kan gå förbi fotbollsplaner nu utan att det gör särskilt ont.
Rutschkanor påverkar mig knappt alls.
Små rektangula tegelbyggnader
med barnteckningar tejpade på insidan av glasdörren
får fortfarande mina tankar att stanna och falla.
Jag är ofta stressad över tiden som går
och allt jag inte gjort
och att att min död är mindre avlägsen för varje år.
Men när jag tänker på fönstret
vet jag att det bra med tid som går.
Jag är inte där längre.

أتذكر لوح زجاج النافذة

بدلا من المنظر

كان متّسخا

أتذكر أنّي كنت أشاهد البيوت أمامي

أشفقتُ على الأشخاص يعيشون هناك

قريبا جدا

أتذكر ملعب كرة القدم

أستطيع أن أمر جانب الملاعب الآن دون أن أشعر بألم كثير

الأرجوحة لا تكاد تؤثر عليَّ

مدارس صغيرة مستطيلة من الطوب

ما زالت تجعل أفكاري أن تتوقف وتسقط

غالبا أشعر بتوتر مع مرور الوقت

وكلّ ما لم أفعلها حتى الآن

وأنّ موتي أقرب وأقرب في كل سنة تمر

ولكن حين أفكر بالنافذة

أعرف أن الوقت الذي يمر هو شيء جيد

فأنا لست هناك الآن

Du förstod inte mina dimensioner
istället tittade du på mina skor
och sa att de var fula
Du såg inte vidden av mina dimensioner
iställade placerade du en brevvåg
på golvet framför mig och sa:
de väger ingenting

لم تُدرك مضموني
فنظرتَ على ملابسي
وقلتَ إنّها قبيحة
لم تفهم مدى قيمتي
وودعتَ ميزانا
على الأرض أمامي وقلتَ
وزنك لا شيء

Kostymen passar inte.
Scenen är upp och ned.
Var dig själv! väser regissören.
Han drar i snörena.
Det rycker i handlederna.

Jag kan replikerna utantill.
Blickar möts enligt schemat.

I salongen ser jag hårfästen.
Jag skriker.
Vilken inlevelse, säger vissa.
Avvikelse från manus, säger andra.
En person tittar upp.
I ögat ser jag spegelbilden
av en skärm där någon
som påminner om mig
skymtar förbi.

لا يناسبني الزيّ

المشهدُ مقلوبٌ

"كوني أنتِ", يزمجر المخرِج

يشدّ الخيوط

فترتجف ذراعيَّ

أردّد النّص عن ظهرِ قلب

تلتقي نظراتنا حسب البرنامجِ

هناك فجوَة بين السؤال والجواب

في الصالة لا أرى الوجوه

أرى هامات الجمهورِ

أصرخ

"ما هذا الاندماج؟ يا للروعة", يقول بعض الجمهور

"هذا خروج عن النصّ", يقول بعض الآخر

شخص يرفع نظره إليَّ

أرى في عينيه

انعكاس خيال

من الشاشة

وفيه لمحة من إمرأةٍ

تشبِهني

Jag vill inte ha något duggregn.
Jag vill gå in i ett moln
och komma ut genomvåt.

لا أريد المطر الخفيف
أريد أن أدخل غيمة
وأخرج مبلّلة

Han ville vara stormen
fälla träd horisonella
se såren i jorden där
rötterna stack upp

Han ville vara stormen
sätta skräck i badgäster
se kaos och flykt
en punkterad badboll
i trädgrenarna

Han ville vara stormen
han grät om någon
kallade honom bris
Vindbyar sågs aldrig
på tevenyheterna

Han sörjde att han inte
kunde skriva sin signatur
på ödelagda hus

Han var bitter över att allt vi
mindes efter hans framfart
var människor tillsammans
som planterade träd och
byggde upp

أراد أن يَكُنَّ العاصفة
ويقطع الأشجار
وينظر إلى الشقوق في الأرض
التي تبرز منها الجذور

أراد أن يَكُنَّ العاصفة
ويخيف السابحين
وينظر إلى الفوضى والهاربين
لعبة السباحة مكسورة
في أغصان الشجرة

أراد أن يَكُنَّ العاصفة
بكى لو شخصا ما
سماه نسيم
فلا تُرى رياحٌ صغيرةٌ
في الأخبار

كان حزينا لأنه لم يستطيع
أن يوقِّع
على بيوت مدمَّرة

كان يشعر بالمرارة لأن كل التي
نتذكره من اكتساحه
هي أفعال الأشخاص
الذين زرعوا سويا
وبنيوا البيوت من جديد

27

När jag tittar på molnen ser jag djur
djur som simmar ute till havs
djur som lever i fjärran land
djur som ingen visste fanns
När du tittar på molnen
ser du moln

حين أنظر إلى الغيوم أرى حيوانات

حيوانات تسبح في البحر

حيوانات تعيش في بلاد بعيدة

حيوانات لا يعلم أحد وجودها

حين تنظر إلى الغيوم

ترى غيوم

Här är vägen till lägenheten
Ta för all del inte bort fimparna
jag bor bara här tillfälligt

Containern med skräp
behöver ni inte flytta på
snart sticker jag härifrån

Måhända att efter
rörläggningen lagades
asfalten ganska slarvligt
men jag ska inte snubbla
under den korta tid
jag bor kvar här

Buckligt och besvärligt
är bra för det ger mig
motivation att ta tag
i flytten till fjärran land

Staketet utanför porten
lutar mer och mer
för varje år

Maskrosorna skjuter upp
försöker spränga asfalten
och precis som jag
komma härifrån

هذا هو الطريق إلى شقتي
لا تحتاج أن تكنس
كي تلَمَّ أعقابَ السجائر
فأعيش هنا مؤقتا

لا تحتاج أن تنقل
الحاوية بالقمامة
فأنا سأنتقل من هنا عمّا قريب

بعد تصليح الماسورة تحت الأرض
الأسفلت وعر
ولكن لا توجد مشكلة
فأنا لن أتعثّر عليه
في الوقت القصير لي هنا

أفضل الطريق أن تكون محفّرة
فهذا يدفعني أن أبدأ
انتقالي إلى البلاد البعيدة

السياج جنب طريق شقتي
يميل أكثر وأكثر كل سنة

الهندباء تبرز على الطريق
هي تحاول أن تفجر الأسفلت
كما أنا أحاول
الخروج من هنا

Frostens klotter har förstört sikten
Genom rutorna ser jag bara det uppenbara
Alla förmågor är frusna
Bara välbekanta tankar travar
Möter tilltal med uppenbara svar

Jag medverkar i världen som
en fjärdedels människa
Och jag mottar för första gången
lovord

Så behaglig du har blivit att prata med.
Äntligen passar du in!

في النوافيذِ صقيعٌ ليليٌّ
يجعل الرؤيةَ ضَبَابِيَّةً وَمُغَبَّرَةً
لا أشاهد سوى البَيِّنِ
مَهَارَاتِي كُلُّهَا مُتَجَمِّدَةٌ
لَا أفكر سوى أفكار مطروقة
لَا أُجِيب سوى أجوبة مُتَوَقَّعة

أنا ألقى العالمَ وأنا مختلفة
كأنَّني ربع شخص
وللأول مرَّة أحصل مديح

مبروك, برافو إليك
الآن المحادثة معك سهلة
أخيرا أنت شخص مُنَاسب لِلعَالمِنَا

33

Vi är skådespelare.
Du spelar rollen som man och
jag spelar rollen som kvinna.
Din rekvisita är mustasch, tobak och självförtroende.
Min rekvisita är klänning, läppstift och omtanke.
Vi spelar våra roller med inlevelse
men din ersättning är högre än min.

نَحنُ مُمَثِّلَانِ
تُؤَدِّي دَورَ الرَّجُلِ وَأُوَدِّي دَورَ المَرأَةِ
مُستَلزَمَاتُكَ هِيَ الشَّارِبُ وَالتَّبغِ وَثِقَةٌ بِنَفسِكَ
مُستَلزَمَاتِي هِيَ الفُستَانِ وَأَحمَرُ الشِّفَاهِ وَالعِنَايَةِ
نُؤَدِّي دَورَانَا بِمُعَايَشَةٍ وَلَكِن تَعويضُكَ أَكثَرُ مِن تَعويضِي

Jag hade varit ute i det fria
Huden hade omfamnat leran
Benen var rispade av taggar
Ansiktet var ristat av tankar
Du sa att jag skulle tvätta bort
släta ut och måla över med
ett jämnt lager beige
du ville avlägsna alla spår
av mig

كنتُ أتجول في البريّة
كان جلدي يعانق الطين
كُنا رجلايَّ تتخدّش من الأشواك
كان وجهي ينحفر بالأفكار
قلتَ أنّني سأغسلني
وأملّس وأدهن وأطمس
بطبقة مستاوية من اللون البيج
أردتَ إزالة كل الآثار
منّي

Jag står på en tågstation.
Jag fryser, jag är otålig.
Jag väntar på tåget som ska ta mig vidare.
Jag har väntat i 35 år.

أقف في محطَّة القطارِ
متجمّدة ونافذة الصبرِ
أنتظر القطار الّذي سيأخذني من هنا
أنا أنتظره منذ خمسٍ وثلاثين سنة

Du säger att du är fantastisk
och jag håller med
Du är så bra som du tror
med reservation för
att du skulle behöva
några små justeringar
Några tankar här och där
kan rättas till
Några ord kan strykas
andra adderas
Du vore helt underbar
om man bara malde
ner dig i atomer och
från grunden byggde
en ny människa

تقول أنك رائع

وأوافق

أنت رائع كما تظن

مع التحفّظ

فقط تحتاج إلى

تغييرات صغيرة

تصليح بعض من أفكارك

وحذف شيء من كلماتك

وأضافة كلمات أخرى

يمكنك أن تكون مثاليا

إذا طُحِنتَ

إلى ذراتك

ومن الذرات

بُنِيَ شخصٌ جديدٌ

du letade efter ditt decimaltal
jag letade efter mitt decimaltal
utan att vi förstod
att vi är två heltal
och mellan oss finns oändligheten

كنتَ تبحث عن رقمك المركب
كنتُ أبحث عن رقمي المركب
دون أن نفهم
أنّنا رقمان مفردان
وبيني وبينك أعداد لانهائية

En försupen soffgrupp.
En kopp förbittrat kaffe.
En skål med sorg.
Sörpla inte!
Under huden ett
tillslutet kranium.
Nåt saknas mellan
ord och tanke.
Tyst och gnissla tänder!
Drick upp din sorg!

أريكة سكرانة
فنجان من القهوة المرّة
كأس من حزن
لا ترشف!
في الجلد توجد
جمجمة مغلقة
يوجد شيء مفقود بين فكر وكلام
إصمتْ وإصّرْ أسنانك!
إشبر حزنك!

Jag trodde att jag var en låda
med träklossar och metalltrådar.
Jag upptäckte att jag var ett piano.

كنتُ أظنُّ أنّني صندوق
بقطعٍ خشبيّةٍ وخيوطٍ معدنيّةٍ
اكتشفتُ أنّني بيانو

Dikter på engelska

April är National Poetry Writing Month (NaPoWriMo).

Jag skriver en dikt om dagen under april månad.
Dikterna utgår från skrivövningar på napowrimo.net
Jag skriver dem på engelska i första hand.

Här delar jag med mig några av dessa dikter.
Du kan ta del av fler april-dikter, varav vissa är översatta till
svenska och somliga även till arabiska, på annaenbom.se/april

Sonnet

I greet the night and fill my cup with wine.
The cloth of stars projects my blissful dream.
Our hands and lips and hearts: a close-knit team.
The stars all gleam just like your eyes. A sign!

I hear your voice: "Let's drink, my Valentine!"
You're here with me: a joy beyond extreme.
The wine, your touch, our love – an endless stream.
More wine! Can't miss a blink. This is divine.

I wake, a naked mess upon the floor.
Your absence hurts more than my aching head.
Why should I live when you have passed away.

I reach for wine. A glass or two or more.
And hear you whisper: "Stop. Don't want you dead."
One day we meet in heaven, not today.

That night

The eyes see no surprise.
The ears hear what they have heard for years.
All this time I waited for that night.
It will not be tonight.

The road

from church to work

the road is snake shaped and dusty
every curve is like the one before
but more bored

never seen beyond the church
probably it looks the same

the sun is an animal
winter-shy
summer-hunting

I have the colour of the road

Most of them

I had friends even though most of them were thieves. I had memories - even though - most of them were dreams.

The sea

The sea is silence.
Early mornings, I pilgrim to the beach.

Early, there is only me on the beach.
Water and horizon is all I see.

The water and I bow to the horizon.
It feels like there is just the sea and me.

"There is just the sea and me"
say thousands of people at that moment.

At that moment there is thousands of people
on beaches around that same sea, praising it like me.

In the same sea thousands have prayed
when losing their lives in the waves.

Losing lives escaping war on the waves.
The sea is silence.

That window

That window
I remember the glass rather then the view
It was stained
I remember looking at the houses on the other side of the road
I felt sorry for the people living there, so near
I remember a football ground
I can walk by football grounds now without feeling much pain
Basketball courts hardly affect me at all
Brick buildings though, with kids' paintings taped to the inside
of the glass door, still makes my thoughts stop and fall
I am often stressed about the years passing, things I have not
done yet and the fact that my death is less distant for every year
But when I think about that window, I know time passing is
good
I am not there anymore

*

At page 18–19 in this book, you can read this poem in Swedish and Arabic

Dynamic

I tried to explain that dynamic is more beautiful
than symmetric. Imagine two circles with the same diameter,
their centres intersect the same line. It is a static sight.
The eye gets bored quickly. Instead, imagine
that one circle is larger than the other. The eye is now
tempted to move from one circle to the other and back.
Tension is created. Movement is created.
If you also move one circle, so that it is no longer
in line with the other, tension increases, movement increases,
beauty increases.

He looked at me and it was clear that he did not comprehend. I
took a step back. How could I explain to him that
dynamic is beautiful? He who builds houses.
He who walks around with a ruler and a spirit level.
He who can see if a surface is oblique by a millimetre.

I realised that it was not worthwhile to continue explaining.
I could not prepare him any more. The journey must begin now.
It is up to him if he wants to come along. I freed my
upper body from the shirt. I dropped the bra to the floor.
A bang was heard when it landed. He looked at me.
From my attempt to explain that dynamic is beautiful,
he had not understood a word. But his eyes understood.
His hands understood.

The moon

After heavy rainfall
the moon is resting
in hundred newborn lakes

I remember words
a thousand whispers
sticked to my mirror

I remember travelling
a train from Rome to Venice
the landscape faded
as darkness became dense
in the window appeared my face
and whispers: like the moon
big, fat and pale with
dents and dips in random places
Venice crumbled and
the travel ceased

I remember reading
Arabic poems, and the phrase

جميل كالقمر

beautiful like the moon
and rain fell and washed
old whispers away
and I whispered to myself
why not

Anna

Listen, your name means merciful and grace.
That's what the internet says, accept it!

No.

Anna means the sun stroking my face
in the morning when I sleep.
Anna means my skin stroking the sunlight in the evening.
Anna means long nights awake. Nights hundred hours each.
Nights of coding, nights of modelling the world I see
and blending it with the world I feel.
Anna means the sun is a circle
and the sky has the colour #87CEEB.
I told the passerine when it landed on the bridge railing.
And she told me her nights are endless too.
She told me there is no use of describing her
with a poem or with code.
Not even a feather of hers can be modelled
not with a million lines.
She told me she knows I will try anyway
because Anna means long nights awake
where two worlds blend.
Blend like water.
Heal like water.

My house

My house.
It is so high that the wind
makes the marigolds on my balcony
bow.

My house.
It is so high that the wind
enters the cracks around the windows
and reminds me of the heat
of your skin.

My house.
It is so high that the bricks
fumble for
the sky.

My house.
The bricks glow in the rain
and the roughness on their surface
appears as pictograms.

My house.
Hieroglyphs in the rain.
Crooked smiles.
Closed eyelids.
Laughing cellulites.

Curtal sonnet

Not far away there's a forest full of life.
Animals don't sip on wine and feel doubt.
They don't look at a meadow and dream.
At the first glance of green, they run into it.
Don't sit by your window on a Saturday night.
Debra, stop sipping on that glass of wine.
Take two glasses and go to your neighbour.
When you ring the bell, your heart beats hard.
Debra, a beating heart is a heart that is alive.
When I open, tell me, 'cause I feel the same.
We're each other's meadows.

Between winter and spring

The frost has drawn the stories of the night
Fractals on the windshield

I forgot my soft drink in the freezer
now it's all frozen and fragile
a touch and it breaks into pieces
That is how my skeleton feels

The grass wears white hats
it crunches under my shoes
I walk fast, hoping to get inside
before my bones fall apart

In the middle of the day
for an hour or two
the grass is green
windshields are clear
the cold air is almost
bearable

In English they call it "prespring"
it means "Why is it bloody winter cold?
Spring is supposed to come!".

In Swedish we call it "vårvinter": spring winter
it means "After the long winter
we get a glimpse of spring.
Let's enjoy the two hours when
the bubbles of our bones
are released!"

The bridge

Are you thinking about the bridge?
Do you fear that it will break?
Every time you see people cross it, are you afraid?
Do you fear the river?
Do you tremble when you see the bridge's legs
surrounded by water?
Do you hear the seagulls howl like untuned saxophones?
Do birds annoy you?
Can you see the sky change colour?
Do you see that a car passed, and the bridge didn't break?
Can you imagine that the bridge finds it delightful
to dip its feet in water?
Perhaps the cold makes the bridge feel more alive?
Is it possible that the bridge has an ability to perceive
the birds' noise as music?
A truck just passed, are you amazed that the bridge still stands?
Are you aware that you are the bridge?

Me and my oud

My oud is like me.
Short and round. Not an ordinary guitar.
Double strings – awesome sound
when strings are tuned, and like my mood
they rarely are.

My oud has no frets.
It is not limited to semitones.
I can play a quartertone, even a
two hundred and fifty-sixth tone
if my fingers are small enough.
Any interval is possible
just like my brain can go
any synapse road untravelled before.

Ebony pegs are considered good
since they make the tuning stay.
My oud has pegs of apricot.
Adjust as much as you want
try to tame the sound
after a second my oud and I
return to the noise
we were born to play.

I will give it shelter

I will give it shelter.
I will make room by the fireplace.

I will let it eat and drink.
It will feel safe, warm and loved.

The fear.
So secure that one day, it's ready to leave the nest.

I am here now

the years surround me like worn out rubber bands
I don't remember what they embraced before they dried
just that they wanted to embrace more

then comes the voice
music is nothing but particles in movement
I have the same body as I had before I pressed play
but I feel like a part has been added
the soul I would call it, if I didn't know better
I wish I didn't know better

it is a schlager
paved and heavily trafficked
sticky ice cream paper in the ditch
but the soul always sees something under the asphalt
during three beats I forget to chase
less travelled paths, I forget to count
how many rubber bands I have left
I am here now
that's enough

Garbage

Cardboard boxes
sleep next to
the lilies. Their
bellies are dampened
by the grass. I
meant to take them
to the dump but
maybe my garbage
loves my garden
as much as I.

Poetry writing prompt

1. Visit an exclusive antique and vintage shop that is called "the dump".
There you will find a broken calfskin drum.

2. On the inside of the drum, write the words that hurt.

3. Play a beat that is rhythmic, but not.

4. See the calf come to life.

5. The calf bows its head to the grass and eats, do the same.

6. Read the lines that the calf's snout and your face has drawn on the ground.
That is the metre of your poem.

7. Follow the calf until your feet feel like hooves on the meadow.
Notice the wind against your skin that has once been a drum.

8. Write down your experience.
The writing should be longer than a life and shorter than a sigh.

9. When dusk comes, go home to the one you miss.
He has emptied the disk washer and cooked a vegan meal.

10. He asks about your writing day and smiles.
Your poem is the wrinkles around his eyes.

Later

Do you want to read my poem?
I can't find the knife.
Do you want to read my poem?
The pasta needs more salt.
Do you want to read my poem?
Later. Let's eat first.
And then some paperwork.
And the floor needs sweeping.
And I need a little nap.
And the dishes are still on the table.
And that email needs to be replied.

Can you turn off the light, good night, by the way, did you say
something about a poem?
I'm sleeping on the sofa. Good f**ing night.

The purpose

Big Bang – 13.8 billion years ago
Life on earth – 3.5 billion years ago
I was born – 38 years ago
Small probabilities times three
There must be a meaning
Sometimes it seems that I was sent as a human to earth
with the purpose of scanning receipts and making sure that
purchases of petrol were booked at account 5611

Small

Smaller than the dot of the i in tiny.
Smaller than a carbon atom in the universe of the dot.
Smaller than the echo of the shadow of the spin of the photon
that takes an electron in the carbon atom to an excited state.
That is how small my problems are.
And still significant for the photon.

Pancakes

The pancakes
Before I stack them,
I fold them
Then I climb
hand in hand
with my dreams
The higher the pancake pile
the more distant seems
the breakfast table of reality
And reason
sitting on a slice of
factory-cut wholemeal bread
and staring at us
gets dizzy
Finally we fall
as we always do
when pancakes are
sufficiently folded
We land on reason
and form a wobbly mess
reason is dreaming
and the dreams are
strengthened by whole grains
So we are ready to
start the day

You say

You say I look old
that I have lines around my eyes and in my forehead
like if a spider web was shattered and stuck in my face.
You say I look pale
as if it has been winter
for five hundred days.
I say your manners are lacking
like a skew rusty bread bin with no bread within.
You say I look old
while your face is so deeply fold
that the Swedish Transport Agency would approve it as a winter
tire.
You say I look pale
while your face is so faded away
that you look like a ghost that has been in the washing machine
for a thousand days.

Diminished triads

Convulsively crawled the mites
along the falling grape leaves,
accompanied by the
diminished triads.

Stumbling fled the man
from the thunder striking,
he with the ravenous hands
and limbs that knew no borders,
accompanied by the
diminished triads.

The smoke ceased,
the life destroying
machines subsided.
The clouds scattered.
A new sky was formed.
While I played the
diminished triads.

Spring cleaning

Love is like spring cleaning.
Everything is the same but different.
The surfaces lay bare.
There is a shimmer above everything.
It smells like a walk in the forest, like standing by the sea.
My nose is addicted to that smell.

Love is like dirtying.
Everything is the same but different.
Like yesterday but more smeared.
Like the day before yesterday but more greasy.

Should I buy a hinge tweaker?
The sunset smells like touch.
I reach out my arms.

Sunsets pass by.
It is neither clean nor dirty.
The poem can't end like this!
It did not turn out like I imagined.
I should have bought that hinge tweaker.

Fibonacci

no
matter
how I try
to fit my poem
into Fibonacci metre
it will never be pure poetry like a pinecone

To the idiot

To the idiot that ruined my life

I hate you
You have stolen the only valuable thing I had: my time
Why did you make me hurry through life to accomplish all
those unnecessary tasks?
Why did you mislead me into chasing for appreciation?
Why did you tell me I am not good enough?

All I have now are lost years and grinded teeth.

*

To the idiot whose life I ruined

Thank you for reminding me of all my faults.
Thank you for reminding me that time is running out.
Thank you for reminding me that I am not good enough.

Your words dig the valleys in my teeth even deeper.

Today

this day is called today
and so we named yesterday
and tomorrow, the same way
we're always stuck in today
a calender orders every day
in a two dimensional array
but in my mind, the days lay
like fallen leaves, all astray
some have withered away
but they all existed, every day
and they all were called today
did I enjoy all of them? no way!
but could I please, if I may
have them all back anyway

Al-Mutanabbi

No one dares to call themselves a rider
after seeing me steering my camel
There is no prouder animal in the world
than a camel that is blessed to carry me
I travel a thousand and one days and nights
at night, my road is lit by the light of my eyes
Dunes float aside to let me pass by
Grains wait in eternity hoping for the honour
to be stepped on by the toe of my camel
"The horse, the night and the desert know me"

Nothing is sharper in the world than my sword
it shines so bright the stars are jealous
No need to pierce or stain it with blood
when I pull it, enemies drop dead by the sight
No one can throw a spear as far as I
I threw it in the 10th century and it still flies
My weapons can kill a dozen in a strike
but deadliest are the words that I write
The M to the I are stronger than dynamite
"The sword, the spear, the notepad and the pen know me"

My words are sublime, higher than the sky
I combine them in ways so bold that grammarians shake
Letters are arranged so they meet for the first time
dazzled and surprised, they bow with a shy smile
When I write, the paper becomes marble
and the ink becomes glowing gold

It does not matter if you lost your sight
it does not matter if you are dead or alive
my writing does not escape anyone's eye
"I am the one whose literature the blind can see"

Storms stop blowing when hearing my poems
Every letter recited makes the air vibrate
the sound waves fill the atmosphere layer
each letter's vibration goes on forever
The sound of my lyrics amaze the nightingale
all the songs and music seem suddenly pale
No matter if your hearing doesn't work
if you are born or in utero waiting for birth
my words resonate in heaven and on earth
"My words were heard by the deaf"

*

The quoted lines come from a poem by Al-Mutanabbi.
More information about that poem at
arabic.fi/poems/2

At the museum

I liked that it had movement
It made me contemplate about
how motion can be really slow
So slow it appears as though
nothing really happens at all

That movement made me think
about the concept of time
How very long a human life
and how painfully short
Full of action and nothing

I loved how it was integrated
Nearly a part of the room
Not located at eye level
Since life brings treasures
in places quite unexpected

Cleverly it had a center
far away from the middle
And small focal points
each of them overly sure
they were the true center

It was surrounded by blur
impossible to distinguish
the boundaries of the core
from the rest of the world
Yes I am you and you are me

Impressive to say the least
About to give highest grade
A strong ten out of ten
Then the museum curator came
and swept the stain away

I am an alchemist

I can no longer see the walls, books cover my hom I have read
everything humans know about the world

I have a broken glass to drink from
and a timeworn pot to cook my meals
all other containers that I own
are reserved for alchemy

I live by the beach, my neighbours are palm trees
moving with the beat of the sea
olives and almonds grow in my garden
but no tree or plant excites me more
than the air that makes them sway

I used to think that air was nothing
just something without colour or taste
that slowed the raindrops down
now I know air is nitrogen, oxygen
and more, I even found some coal

using what is in the air we breathe
I make things the world has never seen
today there is a purple light, yesterday an explosion
no one knows what will happen tomorrow
not even me

I am an artist without pencil or canvas
I create using air and heat
heat is for particles what love is for humans
it makes them warm, makes them come together

the books are ready, waiting to fulfill their duty
of crashing down and die
any second, in my containers
a reaction will occur and it will overturn
all human knowledge

A god in a box

I am a god.
I don't eat at a dining table.
Why would I need a scented candle
when I can set the sky on fire?
I don't care if they come in all colours
if they smell like vanilla or cinnamon
oh they have the coconut scent
that's quite irresistible, I'll take ten.

I am a god.
I sleep on mountains and walk on forests
nothing tickle my toes like tree tops
but for variation I could try a rug
a striped and one with polka dots, why not.
When I have guests we could dine at a table
I'll take a cloth as well and glasses for many
next party we won't have beer from the barrel.

I am a god.
I bring order out of chaos.
Now I'm lost among shelves with night lamps
a mountain of shopping is blocking my sight.
I'm stuck in a big, blue box called IKEA.

I am Thor.
My mother is the earth.
Now her forests are plundered
oil and metals are taken from her
to make and transport all this stuff
while I'm picking another striped rug.

The item

So much junk was found
in the weird widow's house.
It took two days to clean it out.

How about this tiny vase?
asked one of the estate clearance guys.
It's a bit skew, like melting in my hand,
stripes refusing to align.
Can it still smell the scent
of the liquids it has contained?

It's an 80's IKEA item
that can sell for two bucks
or three in our flea market,
not worth the bother,
said his colleague.

No, it's too rough, surely
made by a child or old one
with shaky thumbs,
just throw it, speed up,
said the estate clearance boss.

I haven't yet learned the rule of crookedness,
sometimes it signifies fine art
and sometimes the work of a child.
I just feel the wry whisper of this vase
screaming so loud,
thought the estate clearance guy
while walking to the garbage pile.

Surrounded by marmalade jars
and hangover whiskey glass
broke the 1st century
Roman perfume bottle
and its rose petal heart.

Vill du läsa mer av Anna Enbom?
Besök annaenbom.se

Vill du lära dig arabiska?
Besök arabic.fi